ACHIEVE 100

D1586799

Grammar, Punctuation and Spelling

REVISION

Marie Lallaway

RISING STARS

Acknowledgements

Rising Stars is grateful to the following schools who will be utilising Achieve to prepare their students for the National Tests: Chacewater Community Primary School, Cornwall; Coppice Primary School, Essex; Edgewood Primary School, Notts; Henwick Primary School, Eltham; Norwood Primary School, Southport; Sacred Heart Catholic Primary School, Manchester; Sunnyfields Primary School, Hendon; Tennyson Road Primary School, Luton.

Every effort has been made to trace all copyright holders, but if any have been inadvertently overlooked, the Publishers will be pleased to make the necessary arrangements at the first opportunity.

Although every effort has been made to ensure that website addresses are correct at time of going to press, Rising Stars cannot be held responsible for the content of any website mentioned in this book. It is sometimes possible to find a relocated web page by typing in the address of the home page for a website in the URL window of your browser.

Hachette UK's policy is to use papers that are natural, renewable and recyclable products and made from wood grown in sustainable forests. The logging and manufacturing processes are expected to conform to the environmental regulations of the country of origin.

ISBN: 978 1 78339 541 5

© Rising Stars UK Ltd 2015

First published in 2015 by Rising Stars UK Ltd, part of Hodder Education, an Hachette UK Company

Carmelite House

50 Victoria Embankment

London EC4Y 0DZ

Reprinted 2015

www.risingstars-uk.com

Author: Marie Lallaway

Series Editor: Maddy Barnes

Accessibility Reviewer: Vivien Kilburn

Educational Adviser: Josh Lury

Publishers: Kate Jamieson and Gillian Lindsey

Project Manager: Estelle Lloyd

Editorial: Dodi Beardshaw, Rachel Evans, Amanda George, Fiona Leonard

Cover design: Burville-Riley Partnership

Illustrations by John Storey, Pen and Ink Book Company Ltd

Text design and typeset by the Pen and Ink Book Company Ltd

Printed by Craft Print Pte Limited, Singapore

A catalogue record for this title is available from the British Library.

Contents

Welcome to Achieve Key Stage 2 GPS Revision Book 100

In this book you will find all the activities and information you need to achieve the expected scaled score of 100 in the Key Stage 2 English Grammar, Punctuation and Spelling (GPS) tests.

About the Key Stage 2 Grammar, Punctuation and Spelling National Tests

The tests will take place in the summer term in Year 6. They will be done in your school and will be marked by examiners – not by your teacher.

The tests are divided into two papers:

Paper 1: questions – 45 minutes (50 marks)

- You will answer short questions about grammar, punctuation and language strategies.
- Some questions will ask you to tick a box, circle or underline. Other questions will ask you to add words to a sentence, or to rewrite it making a change. You may be asked to explain why a sentence is written in a particular way.
- The questions will include the language of grammar and punctuation.
- Most questions are worth 1 mark, but you should check to make sure before you answer each question in case you need to give more than one answer.

Paper 2: spelling – approximately 15 minutes (20 marks)

Twenty questions will be read aloud to you, one at a time. You will be asked to spell a particular word in each sentence. Some words may require a correctly placed apostrophe.

- The words may be taken from the word lists for Years 1–6.
- Each correct answer is worth 1 mark.

4

Test techniques

Before the tests

- Try to revise little and often, rather than in long sessions.
- Choose a time of day when you are not tired or hungry.
- Choose somewhere quiet so you can focus.
- Revise with a friend. You can encourage and learn from each other.
- Read the 'Top tips' throughout this book to remind you of important points in answering test questions.
- Make sure that you know what the words in the glossary mean.

During the tests

- READ THE QUESTION AND READ IT AGAIN.
- If you find a question difficult to answer, move on; you can always come back to it later.
- Always answer a multiple-choice question. If you really can't work out the answer, have a guess.
- Read the question again after you have answered it. Check you have done what the question asked you to do.
- If you have any time left at the end, go back to the questions you have missed. If you really do not know the answers, make guesses.

Where to get help:

- Pages 69–70 contain a glossary to help you understand key terms about grammar, punctuation and spelling.
- Pages 71–72 provide the answers to the 'Try this' questions.

How to use this book

1 **Introduction** – This introduces each question strand. Each strand has been broken down into smaller strands to help you. Words in bold can be found at the back of the book in the glossary.

2 **What you need to know** – Important facts are given in this section. Read them carefully. Words in bold are key words and those in lilac are also defined in the glossary at the back of the book.

3 **Let's practise** – This gives an example question for you to read through. Follow the steps carefully and work through the example.

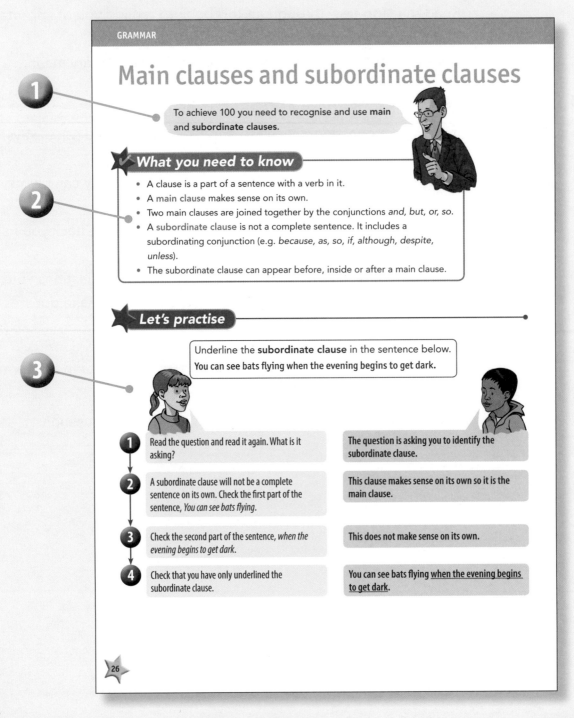

GRAMMAR

Main clauses and subordinate clauses

1 To achieve 100 you need to recognise and use **main** and **subordinate clauses**.

What you need to know

- A clause is a part of a sentence with a verb in it.
- A main clause makes sense on its own.
- Two main clauses are joined together by the conjunctions *and, but, or, so.*
- A subordinate clause is not a complete sentence. It includes a subordinating conjunction (e.g. *because, as, so, if, although, despite, unless*).
- The subordinate clause can appear before, inside or after a main clause.

2

Let's practise

3 Underline the **subordinate clause** in the sentence below.
You can see bats flying when the evening begins to get dark.

1 Read the question and read it again. What is it asking? → The question is asking you to identify the subordinate clause.

2 A subordinate clause will not be a complete sentence on its own. Check the first part of the sentence, *You can see bats flying.* → This clause makes sense on its own so it is the main clause.

3 Check the second part of the sentence, *when the evening begins to get dark.* → This does not make sense on its own.

4 Check that you have only underlined the subordinate clause. → You can see bats flying <u>when the evening begins to get dark</u>.

26

4 Try this – Practise answering the questions for yourself.

 5 Top tips – These hints help you to do your best. Use them well.

 Notebook – Use a notebook or a piece of paper.

GRAMMAR

4

⭐ **Try this**

1 Tick ✔ the box to show the **main clause** in the sentences below.

Although I enjoy going to the cinema, my favourite activity is going to the museum.

My dad came into the room as I was jumping up and down on the sofa.

2 Tick ✔ two boxes to show which of the sentences below contain a **subordinate clause**.

Sentence	Subordinate clause
Freddie can run very well because he practises every day.	
Laura likes to play football and she has a match most weekends.	
When Oscar goes on holiday, he swims in the sea.	

3 Add the correct word to complete the **subordinate clause** in the sentences below.

| although | because | if |

Amy goes to school on a bus _____ she lives too far away to walk.
_____ they are not as popular as rabbits and guinea pigs, snakes make interesting pets.
Could you hang the washing on the line _____ you have time please?

4 Which option correctly introduces the **subordinate clause** in the sentence below? Circle the correct option.

furthermore   in addition   otherwise   even though

Edward wanted to go to school _____ he wasn't feeling very well.

5 Underline the **subordinate clause** in each sentence below.

While you were playing outside, I finished my book.

We will go for a picnic unless it rains.

5

⭐ **Top tips**

• A subordinate clause begins with a subordinating conjunction such as *while, if, when, because* (see pages 24–25 and 29).
• Does the clause make sense on its own? If so, it is a main clause. If not, it is a subordinate clause.

 27

⭐ 7

Nouns

To achieve 100 you need to know what **nouns** are and how to use them.

✔ What you need to know

- There are different types of **nouns**: proper, common, collective and uncountable.
- Proper nouns are easy to spot because they are written with a capital letter. They are the names of people, places and things: Sarah, Mr Smith, Africa, Rising Stars Limited.
- Common nouns, collective nouns and uncountable nouns do not have a capital letter.

Let's practise

Circle two **nouns** in the sentence.

My sister is going to France soon.

1 Read the question and read it again. What is it asking?

The question is asking you to circle two nouns.

2 Look for proper nouns. They begin with capital letters.

France is a proper noun, so circle it.

3 Check for any other nouns by asking whether the words name an object or idea.

The *my* = ✘. The *sister* = ✔. The *is* = ✘. The *to* = ✘. The *soon* = ✘.

4 Check that you have circled two nouns.

①　②
My (sister) is going to (France) soon.

Try this

1 Tick ✔ the box to show the **noun** in the sentence below.

I like to swim in the sea.

2 Underline the three **nouns** in the sentence below.

On Saturdays, we often play in the park or our garden.

3 Add a **noun** to the sentence below.

How many _____ have you got?

! Top tip

- Always check **how many** nouns you are asked to identify.

Adjectives

To achieve 100 you need to know what **adjectives** are and how to use them. You may need to make adjectives from nouns or verbs.

✔ What you need to know

- **Adjectives** describe nouns. They may be in front of the noun (e.g. a *hungry* dog) or after a noun (e.g. the dog is *hungry*).

★ Let's practise

Tick ✔ the box to show the **adjective** in the sentence below.

I found a lost sock under the bed.
↑   ↑   ↑   ↑
☐   ☐   ☐   ☐

1 Read the question and read it again. What is it asking?

The question is asking you to find an adjective.

2 An adjective describes a noun so look for any nouns in the sentence.

Sock and *bed* are nouns.

3 Check if there is an adjective in front of *sock* or *bed*.

Lost describes sock. There is no adjective in front of *bed*. Tick the box below *lost*.

4 Check you have ticked one box.

I found a lost sock under the bed.
↑   ↑   ↑   ↑
☐   ✔   ☐   ☐

★ Try this

1 Circle two **adjectives** in the sentence below.

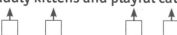
My favourite aunt has a new car.

2 Label the boxes with **N** (noun) and **A** (adjective) to show these types of words.

I love cuddly kittens and playful cats.
↑   ↑   ↑   ↑
☐   ☐   ☐   ☐

3 Complete the sentence below using the word <u>danger</u> as an **adjective**. Remember to punctuate your answer correctly.

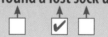
When the river floods, _____

9

Verbs

To achieve 100 you need to know what **verbs** are and how to use them.

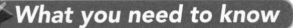

✔ What you need to know

- **Verbs** are actions or states happening now, in the past, or in the future.
- Actions can be things you can see happening (e.g. *run, jump, build, explore, answer*) or they can be 'invisible' actions (e.g. *think, imagine, hear, like, love*).
- Frequently used verbs are *be – am, is, are, was; have – have, has, had.*

★ Let's practise

Underline two **verbs** in the sentence below.

It was my birthday so I visited the zoo yesterday as a treat.

1	Read the question and read it again. What is it asking?	The question is asking you to find two verbs.
2	Look for the easiest verb to spot. This is usually a verb to name an action.	*Visited* is an action. Underline *visited*.
3	Check if there is a verb to describe a state. These are often forms of *have* or *be*.	*Was* is a form of the verb *be*. Underline *was*.
4	Check that you have underlined two verbs.	① ② It <u>was</u> my birthday so I <u>visited</u> the zoo yesterday as a treat.

★ Try this

1 Tick ✔ the box to show the **verb** in the sentence below.

My baby sister sleeps in the afternoon.

⬆ ☐ ⬆ ☐ ⬆ ☐   ⬆ ☐

2 Circle the two **verbs** in the sentence below.

Leaves fall from the trees in autumn but they grow again in the spring.

3 Underline all the **verbs** in the sentences below.

Alisha likes cakes and she is a good baker. Yesterday, she made some lovely buns for us.

★ Top tip

- You may be asked to change the tense of a verb (see page 34 for more information).

Adverbs

To achieve 100 you need to know what **adverbs** are, how to form them and how to use them.

✔ What you need to know

- **Adverbs** are used to describe verbs (e.g. Max will leave *soon*. *Soon* is the adverb that tells us when Max will leave.).
- Many *how* adverbs end in *-ly* but not all. Look out for ones such as work *hard*, run *fast*, drive *straight*.

★ Let's practise

Tick ✔ two boxes to show the **adverbs** in the sentence below.

Later the puppy saw a cat and barked loudly.

	1	Read the question and read it again. What is it asking?	**The question is asking you to find two adverbs.**
2	Look for the easiest adverb to spot. This is usually an adverb to describe how an action is done, and often an *-ly* spelling.	**Loudly describes how an action is done. Tick loudly.**
3	Check if there is an adverb to describe where or when something is done.	**Later tells you when it is done. Tick later.**
4	Check that the other words do not answer the question. Check that you have ticked two boxes.	**Later the puppy saw a cat and barked loudly.**

★ Try this

1 Circle two **adverbs** in the sentence below.

We must move silently to surprise them now.

2 Rewrite this sentence adding an **adverb**. Remember to punctuate your answer correctly.

Let's go home.

_____

! Top tip

- **Watch out:** It's easy to miss common adverbs that refer to *when* something happens: *after, before, later, now, soon, yet.*

11

Modal verbs

To achieve 100 you need to know what **modal verbs** are and how to use them.

What you need to know

- A **modal verb** is a word that tells you how possible, or necessary, an action is (e.g. *might*, *may*, *can*, *will*).
- A modal verb is used together with another verb (e.g. He *can* run. She *might* win.).

Let's practise

Number these sentences to show which is the **most** likely to happen (**1**) to the **least** likely (**3**).

I will go to school today. ☐

I might go swimming on Saturday. ☐

I can come to play later. ☐

1 Read the question and read it again. What is it asking?

The question is testing whether you understand how modal verbs show what is likely to happen.

2 Find the modal verbs from each sentence, so you are ready to compare them.

The modal verbs are *will*, *might*, *can*.

3 Find the sentence which shows the action will definitely happen. Number this as 1.

The modal verb *will* shows this.

4 Check for the modal verb that shows that the action might or might not happen. Number this as 3.

Find the sentence using *might*.

5 Number the last sentence as 2.

can must be 2.

6 Check that you have put the numbers in the correct boxes.

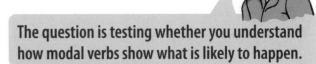

I will go to school today. 1

I might go swimming on Saturday. 3

I can come to play later. 2

 **Try this**

1 Circle one **modal verb** in the sentence below.

If it rains, you **must** bring an umbrella and wear your wellies.

2 Tick ✔ the sentence which is **least** likely to happen.

Tick **one**.

Alex can go to the cinema on Friday. ☐

Sam will bring her sister to the party. ☐

Jo may be singing in the show tonight. ☐

Jaya could arrive at any time. ☐

3 Add a **modal verb** to this sentence.

My brother _____ swim all the way across the pool.

4 Label these sentences to show whether they show **certainty** (C) or **possibility** (P).

Susie will start school when she is four. ☐

Jake might come to our school. ☐

I can swim two lengths of the pool. ☐

5 Rewrite the sentence below by changing the **modal verb** to show that the action will definitely happen. Remember to punctuate your answer correctly.

You might fall if you do that.

_____

6 Tick ✔ the two sentences which each contain a **modal verb**.

Tick **two**.

As I opened the door, everyone shouted, 'Happy Birthday.' ☐

If we all work together, we can be finished by lunchtime. ☐

When Colin arrives, he might show us his new game. ☐

While I was sleeping, my puppy ate my slippers. ☐

Adverbials

To achieve 100 you need to identify and construct an **adverbial**.

What you need to know

- An **adverbial** phrase tells us more about the verb.
- It tells us how, why, when or where an action is done.

Let's practise

Underline the **adverbial phrase** in the sentence below.
A swan has made a nest beside the river.

1	Read the question and read it again. What is it asking?	**The question is asking you to find the adverbial phrase.**
2	First, find the verb by identifying what is done in the sentence.	*Made* **is the verb.**
3	Check if there is any information about how or why it was made.	**No, there is not.**
4	Check if there is any information about when or where it was made.	**There is not any information about** *when*, **but it does tell us** *where* **it was made:** *beside the river.*
5	Check you have underlined all the words of the adverbial phrase.	**A swan has made a nest** <u>beside the river</u>.

Top tip

- Use the same method each time so that you don't forget one of the questions to ask about the sentence, e.g. *How? Why? When? Where?*

 **Try this**

1 Tick ✔ two boxes to show the sentences below that contain **adverbial phrases**.

Tick **two**.

They love watching funny cartoons. ☐

Later that day we all shared a pizza. ☐

We ran as fast as we could. ☐

Our television is broken. ☐

2 Circle the **adverbial phrase** in the sentence below.

We hope to see you by the end of the month.

3 Tick one box to show which part of the sentence is an **adverbial**.

Everyone in our class has brought a picnic to eat in the new nature garden.

☐ ☐ ☐ ☐

4 Rewrite the sentence below moving the **adverbial** to the end. Remember to punctuate your answer correctly.

More slowly than a snail, Josh put on his coat.

_____

5 Tick ✔ one box in each row to show whether the adverbial tells you **when** or **where** something happens in the sentences below.

Sentence	When?	Where?
I'll meet you outside the swimming pool.		
Can you come at three o'clock?		
After you have eaten your lunch, shall we play football?		
Alisha clapped her hands at the same time as her sister.		

Pronouns

To achieve 100 you need to know what **pronouns** are and how to use them.

✓ What you need to know

- **Pronouns** are words that take the place of nouns in a sentence. They help to avoid repeating the same words. There are different types of pronouns:
  - Personal pronouns:
    - *I, you, he, she, it, we, they* (used as the subject of a sentence)
    - *me, you, him, her, it, us, them* (used as the object of a sentence)
  - Possessive pronouns:
    - *mine, yours, his, hers, its, ours, theirs*

Let's practise

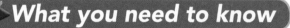

> Underline two **pronouns** in the passage below.
>
> **Louis went to the swimming pool with his best friend. They had a great time.**

 1 Read the question and read it again. What is it asking?

The question is asking you to find two pronouns in the passage.

2 Find the words that are used instead of a noun.

His is used instead of *Louis* and *They* is used instead of *Louis* and *best friend*.

3 Check that the other words do not answer the question. Check that you have underlined two pronouns.

Louis went to the swimming pool with <u>his</u> **①** best friend. <u>They</u> **②** had a great time.

! Top tips

- You can decide if a word is a pronoun by testing whether you can replace it with a noun.
- **Watch out:** Remember that *I* and *my* are pronouns. These ones are often overlooked.

 **Try this**

1 Tick ✔ two boxes to show the sentences that contain **pronouns**.

Tick **two**.

Mr White has two cats. ☐

I love my pet rat. ☐

The children ate their lunches outside. ☐

The elephants were spraying water everywhere. ☐

2 Circle all the **pronouns** in this sentence.

While you were watching television, I made your supper.

3 Rewrite the sentence below using a **pronoun**. Remember to punctuate your answer correctly.

Ben plays football.

_____

4 Which pair of **pronouns** correctly completes the sentence below?

The car wouldn't start so _____ had to ask someone to help _____.

Tick **one**.

I   my   ☐

we   us   ☐

you   my   ☐

they   our   ☐

5 Add the correct **pronouns** to this passage.

On my birthday, _____ received a present to share with _____ sister. _____ both loved it.

6 Underline all the **pronouns** in the passage below.

John had a new bike. He lent it to his cousin but unfortunately he fell off it because it was too big for him.

Prepositions

To achieve 100 you need to identify **prepositions** and be able to use them.

What you need to know

- A **preposition** is a word that often gives information about time or place.
- The different types of preposition are:
  - prepositions of time: *after, at, before, by, for, to, until*
  - prepositions of place: *at, above, by, between, beside, from, into, onto, next, to, through*
  - other common prepositions: *of, for, off*
- Prepositions are followed by a noun or noun phrase (e.g. *on the table, behind a damaged statue*).

Let's practise

Circle two **prepositions** in the sentence below.
When we get on the bus, you can sit beside me.

1 Read the question and read it again. What is it asking?

The question is asking you to find two prepositions.

2 Find the words that give information about place or time.

Places described are *on the bus* and *beside me.*

3 Identify the words that show 'where' someone is. Check that you have circled two words.

1　　　　　　　**2**

When we get on the bus, you can sit beside me.

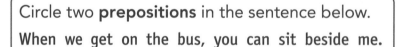

 **Try this**

1 Underline two **prepositions** in the sentence below.

Chris will be coming to our house on your birthday.

2 Tick ✔ two boxes to show the **prepositions** in the sentence below.

I'll meet you after your basketball match so please stand by the door.

↑ ↑ ↑ ↑
☐ ☐ ☐ ☐

3 Add a suitable **preposition** to the sentence below.

A rabbit has dug a tunnel _____ our fence.

4 Circle all the **prepositions** in the sentence below.

Grace travelled to France by plane and stayed in a lovely hotel.

5 Add the most suitable **prepositions** from the box to the sentence below.

| at   in   of   on   over   under |

Mum wanted a bunch _____ flowers to put _____ the table.

6 Rewrite the sentence below changing the **preposition**. Remember to punctuate your answer correctly.

Please put the boxes under the table.

_____

7 Circle all the **prepositions** in the sentence below.

There is a pile of books under the chair beside the window.

8 Add a suitable **preposition** to the sentence below.

Please put your coat _____ the peg.

Determiners

To achieve 100 you need to know what **determiners** are and how to use them.

✔ *What you need to know*

- A **determiner** is a word that shows whether you are referring to a noun in general or in particular. It usually comes at the beginning of a noun phrase.
- There are lots of different determiners but the ones you need to know are:
  - *a* words: *a, an, any*
  - *th* words: *the, that, this, these, those*
  - quantity words: *all, some, any, much, more, many*

★ *Let's practise*

Circle four **determiners** in the sentence below.
The horses in this field are quite friendly but some of those ponies do bite.

1 Read the question and read it again. What is it asking? | The question is asking you to find four determiners.

2 Look for determiners beginning with *a*. | There are none of those.

3 Check for determiners beginning with *th*. Make sure they are determiners, not just *th* spellings e.g. *theatre*. | *The, this, those*

4 Find determiners that refer to quantity. | *some*

5 Check that you have found and circled four determiners. | (The) horses in (this) field are quite friendly but (some) of (those) ponies do bite.

! *Top tip*

- Remember that *an* is used in front of a word beginning with a vowel: *a e i o u* or a silent *h* (an hour).

Try this

1. Add the correct **determiners** to the sentence below.

   Please can I have _____ apple, _____ banana or _____ orange for my lunch?

2. Tick ✔ the box to show which **determiners** are used in the sentence below.

   Berta needs some eggs for the cake she is making.

   Tick **one**.

for	she	☐
eggs	is	☐
needs	making	☐
some	the	☐

3. Underline the **determiners** in the sentence below.

   I can't find any coloured pencils in the box, but I have found these three coloured pens.

4. Add a **determiner** to the sentence below.

   Tom has _____ younger brothers.

5. Tick ✔ the boxes to show the **determiners** in the sentence below.

   Lucy would like more cake but there is only a little bit left.
      ↑   ↑   ↑ ↑
      ☐   ☐   ☐☐

Top tips

- Check sentences carefully. It is easy to miss a determiner as we don't really notice them when we speak or read.
- First check for *a* or *an*. Then, check for words beginning with *th* (but make sure they are determiners not just *th* spellings). Next, look for words referring to quantity.

21

Statements, exclamations, commands and questions

To achieve 100 you need to recognise and use **statement**, **exclamation**, **command** and **question** sentences.

What you need to know

- A **statement** gives information. It always ends with a full stop.
- An **exclamation** expresses an emotion, such as surprise or joy. It begins with *How* or *What* and ends with an exclamation mark.
- A **command** orders someone to do something. It begins with a verb.
- A **question** asks someone for information, or to do something. It ends with a question mark and often includes a question word (e.g. *what*, *when*, *where*, *who*, *why*, *how*).

Let's practise

Draw lines to show whether the sentence is a **statement**, **exclamation**, **command** or **question**.

statement	When will you help me?
exclamation	What a lovely present!
command	Tidy up the class now.
question	If you wait, I'll walk with you.

1 Read the question and read it again. What is it asking?

The question is asking you to identify and match types of sentences.

2 Read each sentence in an expressive voice. Which sentences sound like a question or an exclamation? Use the punctuation marks to help you.

What a lovely present! ends with an exclamation mark so must be an exclamation. *When will you help me?* has a question word and ends with a question mark so must be a question.

3 Look for a command. Look for a verb starting the sentence.

Tidy up is a verb. *Tidy up the class now.* is a command.

4 Finally, check that the last sentence is a statement, and that each sentence type is matched up.

statement — When will you help me?
exclamation — What a lovely present!
command — Tidy up the class now.
question — If you wait, I'll walk with you.

Try this

1 Write **C** for **command** or **S** for **statement** in each box for the sentences below.

Now, please listen to the music. ☐

My computer is not working. ☐

It will be rainy today. ☐

Remember to bring your coats with you. ☐

2 Write a **question** for this **answer**.

_____ Yes, please.

3 Write this **question** as a **command**. Remember to punctuate your answer correctly.

Can you open the window?

_____

4 Write a **statement** to answer this **question**. Remember to punctuate your answer correctly.

What will you do tomorrow?

_____

5 Add a **question mark ?** or **exclamation mark !** to the sentences below.

How awful _____

How do you do _____

What do you think _____

What a day _____

6 Change this **command** to a **question**. Remember to punctuate your answer correctly.

Tell me your name.

_____

Top tips

- **Watch out:** Not all sentences with *what, which,* etc. are questions (e.g. *What a super goal!* or *I know why apples fall from trees.*).
- Read the sentences in an expressive voice – like a character in a story. Do this in your head.

Conjunctions

To achieve 100 you need to know the different **conjunctions** and be able to use them.

✓ What you need to know

- **Conjunctions** join clauses.
- The different types of conjunction are:
  - **coordinating conjunctions:** *and, or, but, so*
  - **subordinating conjunctions:** *because, as, so, if, although, despite, unless, when, after, before, while, since, until, during, once, where*

★ Let's practise

Circle the **conjunction** in the sentence below.
Bees come to our garden because there are lots of plants they like.

1 Read the question and read it again. What is it asking?

The question is asking you to find a conjunction.

2 Look at how the sentence is made of two parts (clauses). Find the word which joins the two parts.

Bees come to our garden is part one. Part two is *there are lots of plants they like. because* joins the two parts.

3 Circle the conjunction.

Bees come to our our garden(because)there are lots of plants they like.

! Top tips

- A conjunction is usually found near the middle of a sentence, or at the beginning.
- Look out for the two parts of a sentence and find the word that joins them together.

 **Try this**

1 Add the most suitable **conjunction** from the box to the sentence below.

| unless   while   if   where |

Tom was playing by the pond _____ Alex was digging in the sand pit.

2 Tick ✔ the box to show the **conjunction** in the sentence below.

The whole family went to the beach although it was a freezing cold day.
    ↑   ↑   ↑   ↑
    ☐   ☐   ☐   ☐

3 Write a **coordinating conjunction** to complete the sentence below.

Charlie and I spend a lot of time together _____ we are very good friends.

4 Tick ✔ the boxes to show which sentences contain **subordinating conjunctions**.

We can play in the garden when we get home.   ☐

Can you sing while you are playing the guitar?   ☐

Let's go to the sea and swim.   ☐

If you jump in the pool first, I will follow you.   ☐

5 Add a **subordinating conjunction** to the sentence below.

The cat would not come down from the tree _____ it was frightened of the dog.

6 Underline two **conjunctions** in this sentence.

I have lived here since I was born so I know a lot of people on my street.

7 Add two **subordinating conjunctions** to the sentence below.

_____ you are my best friend, sometimes I like to play with Sajad

_____ he likes to climb trees and you don't.

25

Main clauses and subordinate clauses

To achieve 100 you need to recognise and use **main** and **subordinate clauses**.

What you need to know

- A clause is a part of a sentence with a verb in it.
- A **main clause** makes sense on its own.
- Two main clauses are joined together by the conjunctions *and, but, or, so*.
- A **subordinate clause** is not a complete sentence. It includes a subordinating conjunction (e.g. *because, as, so, if, although, despite, unless*).
- The subordinate clause can appear before, inside or after a main clause.

Let's practise

Underline the **subordinate clause** in the sentence below.
You can see bats flying when the evening begins to get dark.

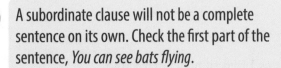

1 Read the question and read it again. What is it asking?

The question is asking you to identify the subordinate clause.

2 A subordinate clause will not be a complete sentence on its own. Check the first part of the sentence, *You can see bats flying*.

This clause makes sense on its own so it is the main clause.

3 Check the second part of the sentence, *when the evening begins to get dark*.

This does not make sense on its own.

4 Check that you have only underlined the subordinate clause.

You can see bats flying <u>when the evening begins to get dark</u>.

Try this

1 Tick ✔ the box to show the **main clause** in the sentences below.

Although I enjoy going to the cinema, my favourite activity is going to the museum.

My dad came into the room as I was jumping up and down on the sofa.

2 Tick ✔ two boxes to show which of the sentences below contain a **subordinate clause**.

Sentence	Subordinate clause
Freddie can run very well because he practises every day.	
Laura likes to play football and she has a match most weekends.	
When Oscar goes on holiday, he swims in the sea.	

3 Add the correct word to complete the **subordinate clause** in the sentences below.

| although   because   if |

Amy goes to school on a bus _____ she lives too far away to walk.

_____ they are not as popular as rabbits and guinea pigs, snakes make interesting pets.

Could you hang the washing on the line _____ you have time please?

4 Which option correctly introduces the **subordinate clause** in the sentence below? Circle the correct option.

furthermore   in addition   otherwise   even though

Edward wanted to go to school _____ he wasn't feeling very well.

5 Underline the **subordinate clause** in each sentence below.

While you were playing outside, I finished my book.

We will go for a picnic unless it rains.

Top tips

- A subordinate clause begins with a subordinating conjunction such as *while, if, when, because* (see pages 24–25 and 29).
- Does the clause make sense on its own? If so, it is a main clause. If not, it is a subordinate clause.

Relative clauses

To achieve 100 you need to recognise and use **relative clauses**.

✓ What you need to know

- A **relative clause** adds extra information about a noun or **noun phrase**. The sentence makes sense without it.
- A relative clause on its own is not a complete sentence.
- It often begins with *who, which, when, where, that*.
- A relative clause is a type of subordinate clause.

★ Let's practise

Underline the **relative clause** in the sentence below.

My new kittens, who are called Smokey and Smudge, sometimes climb up the curtains.

1 Read the question and read it again. What is it asking?

The question is asking you to identify the relative clause.

2 A relative clause adds information about a noun but will not make sense on its own. Look for a clause that does not make sense on its own.

The clause between the commas, *who are called Smokey and Smudge*, adds information about the kittens and does not make sense on its own.

3 Check that you have only underlined the subordinate clause.

My new kittens, <u>who are called Smokey and Smudge</u>, sometimes climb up the curtains.

★ Try this

1 Circle the **relative clause** in the sentence below.

Mikey won a trophy, which was a large silver cup, at his athletics competition.

2 Add a **relative clause** to the sentence below.

My best friend, _____, is great fun to play with.

3 Underline the **relative clause** in the sentence below.

The red bicycle that was left outside the shop belongs to Martin.

Subordinating and coordinating conjunctions

To achieve 100 you need to recognise and use **subordinating** and **coordinating conjunctions**.

✔ What you need to know

- Conjunctions join ideas within a sentence.
- Coordinating conjunctions (e.g. *and*, *but*, *or*) join two main clauses.
- Subordinating conjunctions (e.g. *because*, *as*, *so*, *if*, *although*, *despite*, *unless*) join a main clause and a subordinate clause.

Let's practise

Circle the **conjunction** in the sentence below.
Gina was doing her homework while she was listening to the radio.

1	Read the question and read it again. What is it asking?	The question is asking you to identify the conjunction.
2	Find the clauses in the sentence by identifying which parts make sense on their own.	*Gina was doing her homework* and *she was listening to the radio* both make sense on their own.
3	Find the word that joins the two clauses.	*while*
4	Check that you have circled the conjunction.	Gina was doing her homework (while) she was listening to the radio.

Try this

1 Underline the **conjunction** in the sentence below.

   Hester is trying to learn to play the piano although she is finding it difficult.

2 Write one **conjunction** from the box to complete each sentence below. Each conjunction may be used only once.

   | unless   if   even though |

   The birds will fly away _____ you make too much noise.

   Cows can be dangerous _____ they are often quite friendly.

   My hamster will not come out _____ you are very quiet.

Noun phrases

To achieve 100 you need to recognise and use **noun phrases**.

✔ What you need to know

- A noun phrase includes the noun and any adjectives to describe it. A noun phrase gives detail to a noun. The determiner (e.g. *the, a* or *an*) is part of the noun phrase.
- Information about the noun can appear in front of or after the noun, or in both places.

★ Let's practise

Circle the **noun phrase** in the sentence below.

I have an annoying little brother.

1	Read the question and read it again. What is it asking?	The question is asking you to find the noun phrase.
2	Find the noun.	*Brother* is the noun.
3	Find the words which add information about *brother*. Don't forget the determiner.	*An annoying* and *little* refer to *brother*. *An* is the determiner.
4	Check you have circled the noun phrase.	I have (an annoying little brother.)

✎ Try this

1 Tick ✔ the words that make the **noun phrase** in the sentence below.

We made a beautiful cream cake today.

☐ ☐ ☐ ☐　☐ ☐ ☐

2 Add your own words to the sentence below to expand the **noun phrase**.
Dino has a _____ _____ game.

3 Underline the longest possible **noun phrase** in the sentence below.
The shed at the end of the garden is quite creepy.

Subject and object

To achieve 100 you need to find the **subject** and **object** in sentences.

What you need to know

- All sentences contain a **subject**. This tells you *who* or *what* <u>does</u> the action.
- Some sentences contain an **object**. The object is *who* or *what* the action <u>is done to</u>.
- There can be more than one subject and more than one object in a sentence.

Let's practise

Write **S** (**subject**) or **O** (**object**) in two boxes for the sentence below.

Bethan trains her dog every day.

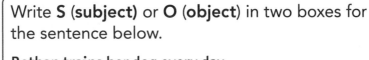

1	Read the question and read it again. What is it asking?	The question is asking you to find the subject and the object.
2	Find the subject by asking yourself who or what is doing the action.	*Bethan* is doing the training so she is the subject. Write *S* in the box below *Bethan*.
3	Find the object by asking who or what is being trained.	The *dog* is being trained. Write *O* in the box below *dog*.
4	Check you have written in two boxes.	Bethan trains her dog every day.

Try this

1 Tick ✔ the table to show which sentences below have an **object**.

Sentence	Object
Joshua sings in class.	
Yuri plays tennis.	
We visit our cousins at the weekend.	

2 Circle the **object** in the sentence below.

Sarah won a prize yesterday.

Subject and verb agreement

To achieve 100 you need to make the **subject and verb** in a sentence agree.

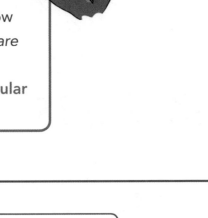

What you need to know

- In the present tense, regular verbs change according to how many people are doing them (e.g. I *am* eating dinner. We *are* eating dinner.).
- To be correct, you must know the difference between **singular** (just one) and **plural** (more than one) subjects.

Let's practise

Circle the correct words to complete the sentences below.

Miss Bennett <u>is / are</u> talking to the class.

Our team <u>is / are</u> trying hard to win the competition.

New flowers <u>is / are</u> appearing each day.

1 Read the question and read it again. What is it asking?

The question is asking you to choose the correct verb form to agree with the subject.

2 Decide whether the subject is singular or plural.

Miss Bennett = 1 person, so singular.

3 If the noun refers to a group, it is likely to use a singular verb form.

Our team = 1 team, so singular.

4 Check if the noun refers to a number of things, *1 flower, 2 flowers*.

Flowers are plural, so use the plural form, *flowers are . . .*

5 Check that you have circled a word for each sentence.

Miss Bennett (is) / are talking to the class.

Our team (is) / are trying hard to win the competition.

New flowers is / (are) appearing each day.

 **Try this**

1 Circle the correct words for the sentence below.

John **is / are** a fast runner so our school **win / wins** the championship each year.

2 Cicle the correct form of the **verb** to complete the sentence.

My family **prefer / prefers** tea to coffee.

3 Tick ✔ the sentences below that are correct.

The children is happy about the holidays. ☐

Beth and Ben want to be scientists. ☐

Wales is a country next to England. ☐

Police officers has arrested the burglar. ☐

4 Circle the correct **subject** to match the **verb** in this sentence.

We / He always goes to bed at 8 o'clock.

5 Match each **subject** with two correct **verbs**.

eat

it
they

believe
grows
does

! **Top tips**

- Look out for nouns that refer to a set of things (e.g. a class, a collection, a government). *A family* contains more than one person but it refers to one family so it is singular, so *My family is going on holiday* not *My family are going on holiday*.
- One person or thing + another person or thing = plural (e.g. *Joe likes boats. Joe and Sam like boats.*).

Verbs in the simple present and simple past tenses

To achieve 100 you need to recognise the simple **present** and simple **past tenses** and be able to construct these verb forms.

 What you need to know

- The **past tense** tells us when something has happened.
- The **present tense** tells us when something is happening.
- Verbs change tenses to show these differences in time.
- Most verbs have similar spellings (e.g. *watch, watched*; *stay, stayed*; *walk, walked*) but there are also irregular verbs (e.g. *go, went*).

Let's practise

> Write the **verbs** in the sentence below in the **past tense**.
>
> | to arrive | | to do |
> | --- | --- | --- |
>
> When Zak _____ home from school, he _____ his homework.

① Read the question and read it again. What is it asking?

The question is asking you to write the verbs in the past tense.

② Look at the first verb, *to arrive*. What is the past tense of *to arrive*?

First, imagine the action happening in the past, e.g. yesterday. The past tense of *arrive* is *arrived*.

③ The next verb is *to do*. What is the past tense of *to do*?

The past tense of *do* or *does* is *did*.

④ Check that you have answered both parts of the question.

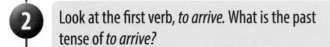

to arrive

When Zak ___arrived___ home from school,

to do

he ___did___ his homework.

 **Try this**

1 Circle two verbs in the **simple past tense** in the sentence below.

At the party, the children played games, danced to music and they are now taking home plenty of cake.

2 Write the verb in the gap in the **simple past tense**.

to visit

Last year, we _____ Scotland for our holiday.

3 Rewrite the sentence below in the **simple present tense**. Remember to punctuate your answer correctly.

Anna had two cats.

_____

4 Circle all the verbs in the **simple past tense** in the passage below.

We usually go to France in the summer but last year we went to Wales. We climbed hills and bathed in the sea. I hope we will go again sometime.

5 Circle the correct **verb form** for the gap in the sentence below.

win / won / is winning / was winning

My basketball team _____ the championship last year.

6 Which pair of **verb forms** correctly completes the sentence below?

Every time Kate _____ to sleep, her brother _____ her jump by banging the door.

Tick **one**.

went	made	☐
is going	has made	☐
go	is making	☐
goes	make	☐

Verbs in the progressive and perfect tenses

To achieve 100 you need to recognise the **present** and **past progressive tenses** and the **present** and **past perfect tenses** and be able to construct these verb forms.

✔ What you need to know

- Progressive tenses refer to an action that is continuous (e.g. I *am reading* this book at the moment.).
- Progressive tenses are made of two parts: the verb 'to be' + a verb ending in -*ing*.
  - **present progressive** = I *am running*; you *are skipping*; he, she or it *is jumping*; we or they *are hopping*.
  - **past progressive** = I *was reading*; you *were writing*; he, she or it *was watching*; we or they *were looking*.
- Perfect forms have two parts. The **present perfect tense** refers to an activity that begins in the past and continues in the present (e.g. *We have lived here for five years.*). The **past perfect tense** shows that one action has happened before another when both are in the past (e.g. *I had seen you before you saw me.*).

★ Let's practise

Circle the correct tense to complete the sentence below.

Katie **played / is playing** outside at the moment.

1 Read the question and read it again. What is it asking? | The question is asking you to choose the correct verb tenses.

2 Look for clues in the sentence that show you when the actions are happening. | *at the moment* = present

3 Chose the present form of the verb. | *played* = past, *is playing* = present

4 Check your answer. | Katie **played** / **is playing** outside at the moment.

 **Try this**

1 Tick ✔ the table to show which sentences below are written using the **present progressive tense**.

Sentence	Present progressive
Archie is cooking tea for us.	
Lucy wants to make a drink.	
The children are waiting for their teacher.	
We will arrive home tomorrow.	

2 Underline the verb in the sentence below in the **present perfect** tense.

We moved to the country three years ago and we have lived here since then.

3 Tick ✔ one box to show the correct **verb** to complete the sentence below.

While you _____ the film, I drew a picture for you.

Tick **one**.

watch ☐

were watching ☐

is watching ☐

watches ☐

4 Write the verb in the gap in the **present progressive** form.

| to learn |
↓

The twins _____ to play the guitar.

5 **First Jack missed but then he scored a goal.**

Add one word to the sentence below to show that the actions happened in this order.

Jack _____ missed his first attempt at goal, but then he succeeded.

6 Tick ✔ one box in each row to show whether the sentences below are written in the **present** or **past progressive** form.

Sentence	Present progressive	Past progressive
Rob and Jamie are winning the game.		
Shannon was jumping up and down with excitement.		
My kittens were climbing up the curtains.		
I am hiding under the table.		

Passive and active voices

To achieve 100 you need to recognise the **active** and **passive voices**.

✔ What you need to know

- Most sentences are written in the **active voice** (e.g. *George broke the window.*). They follow a subject + verb + object order (see page 31).
- Sometimes, a different word order is used: object + verb + subject (e.g. *The window was broken by George* or *The window was broken*). This is called the **passive voice**.
- The passive voice is used when:
  - the writer wants to focus on the object (e.g. *the window*);
  - the writer doesn't want to tell who did the action (e.g. *George*);
  - the person is unknown (e.g. *A vase was mysteriously broken*);
  - it doesn't matter who did it (e.g. *The ball was kicked into the net*).

★ Let's practise

Tick ✔ two boxes to show the sentences that are written in the **passive voice**.

Tick **two**.

1 Josh has organised the teams for sports' day. ☐
2 Games have been organised for the party. ☐
3 Sports teams were organised by Josh. ☐
4 Teams report at the start of the competition. ☐

1 Read the question and read it again. What is it asking?

The question is asking you to identify sentences in the passive voice.

2 Identify the subject of each sentence.

1 Josh   2 Games   3 Sports teams   4 Teams

3 Decide if the action is active (subject + verb + object) or passive (object + verb + subject).

1 *Josh has organised* = ACTIVE.
2 *Games* – it is not known who organised them = PASSIVE.
3 *Sports teams* – they were organised by Josh = Josh is after the verb = PASSIVE.
4 *Teams report* = ACTIVE.

4 Tick the two sentences that are in the passive voice. Then check your answer.

2 Games have been organised for the party. ✔
3 Sports teams were organised by Josh. ✔

 **Try this**

1 Tick ✔ one box to show the sentence below that is in the **passive voice**.

Tick **one**.

Oscar drew a super picture. ☐

I love watching films. ☐

The cats played with a ball of string. ☐

Trees had been knocked over by the wind. ☐

2 Tick ✔ a box in each row to show whether the sentence is **active** or **passive**.

Sentence	Active	Passive
Lola was playing tennis.		
The whole class loves basketball.		
The football match has been won by my class.		
Many children in school want to learn to play rugby.		

3 Rewrite the sentence below in the **passive voice**. Remember to punctuate your answer correctly.

Hameed won the prize.

_____

Top tip

• Identify a passive sentence by checking who or what did the action. If the person (or thing) is not given in the sentence, it is passive. If the person (or thing) appears after the verb, it is a passive sentence.

Subjunctive verb forms

To achieve 100 you need to recognise verbs in the **subjunctive form**.

 What you need to know

- The **subjunctive verb form** can be used when the speaker suggests or recommends something and wants to sound formal.
- The subjunctive can be used in sentences that suggest or recommend (e.g. *I suggest that…*; *He recommends that…*; *She advises that…*; *We insist that…*).
- The subjunctive often uses the verb *to be* in an unusual way (e.g. *If I were you…* or *I wish I were stronger…*).

Let's practise

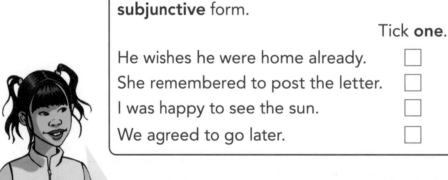

Tick ✔ the sentence below that is in the **subjunctive** form.

Tick **one**.

He wishes he were home already.	☐
She remembered to post the letter.	☐
I was happy to see the sun.	☐
We agreed to go later.	☐

1 Read the question and read it again. What is it asking?

The question is asking you to find a sentence in the subjunctive form.

2 Check for the popular subjunctive verb forms: *If (I) were you* or *(I) wish (I) were.*

The first sentence includes *He wishes he were*, so tick this.

3 Check that there is not another possible answer. Check that all the other verbs agree in the normal way.

She remembered, I was and *We agreed* are used in the normal way.

4 Check you have ticked the box to show the sentence in the subjunctive form.

He wishes he were home already. ✔

Try this

1 Circle the **subjunctive** form to complete the sentence below.

Olivia recommended that Sam <u>sign</u> / <u>signs up</u> for the school basketball team.

2 Underline the verb in the **subjunctive** form in the sentence below.

Her teacher suggested that Lucy arrive on time for her appointment with the head teacher.

3 Tick ✔ one box to show the sentence that is written using the **subjunctive** form.

Tick **one**.

If you look in the cupboard, you will find your pencils. ☐

If I were you, I would save a little money each month. ☐

If you give me your hand, I'll help you cross the road. ☐

If I find your pencil case, I will tell you. ☐

4 Complete this sentence using the **subjunctive** form. Choose one verb from the box below.

| am   is   was   were |

If I _____ you, I would start again with a new pen.

5 Rewrite the verb underlined in the sentence below so that it uses the **subjunctive** mood.

We suggest that he <u>starts</u> the test again.

_____

6 Write the verb in the gap below so that it uses the **subjunctive** mood.

| to be |
↓

I wish I _____ able to come to your party, but I am afraid that I will be busy.

Standard English and formality

To achieve 100 you need to know how to identify **Standard English**, and to recognise differences between informal and formal language.

 What you need to know

- Standard English is the form of the English language widely accepted as the usual correct form. It includes both vocabulary and sentence structures.
- People may use other expressions in speaking or informal writing, but Standard English is used for formal communication.
- You will need to be aware of non-Standard English variations that may be frequently used in your region of the country.

Let's practise

Circle the options that will complete the sentences using **Standard English**.

I <u>was</u> / <u>were</u> late for school.

You'd better run <u>quick</u> / <u>quickly</u>.

1 Read the question and read it again. What is it asking?

The question is asking you to identify Standard English.

2 Read each sentence in your head, trying out both options. Identify the form that would be most commonly found written in a text book.

I was sounds more correct than *I were*. *Quickly* is an adverb that fits with the verb 'run'. *Quick* is an adjective and does not fit with the verb.

3 Check you have circled the correct words.

(I was) / were late for school.
You'd better run quick / (quickly)

1 Tick ✔ the table to show whether the underlined words in each sentence are **Standard English** or **non-Standard English**.

Sentence	Standard English	non-Standard English
Jane <u>ain't</u> coming.		
Hugh <u>was</u> ill yesterday.		
I <u>done</u> my chores this morning.		
We would like <u>them</u> ones, please.		

2 Circle the more **formal** option to complete each sentence.

We must **<u>attempt</u> / try** to make this work.

The police will **<u>look into</u> / investigate** the theft

3 Rewrite the sentence below using **Standard English**. Remember to punctuate your answer correctly.

I haven't done nothing wrong.

_____

Top tip

• Test questions may ask you to circle or underline a Standard English option or to change non-Standard to Standard English. You may also be asked to select more formal language from a choice of options.

Capital letters, full stops, exclamation marks and question marks

To achieve 100 you need to use **capital letters**, **full stops**, **exclamation marks** and **question marks** in the right places in sentences.

What you need to know

- Every sentence begins with a **capital letter** and ends with a **full stop**, **exclamation mark** or **question mark**. (See page 22 for more information about questions and exclamations.)
- Proper nouns require a capital letter (e.g. for names of places, people, nationalities, days and months and brand names).

Let's practise

Add the correct **capital letters** and **full stops** to the passage below.

the dragon stepped out of its cave it opened its mouth and gave a fiery breath

1 Read the question and read it again. What is it asking?

The question is asking you to find beginnings and endings of sentences.

2 Read the passage carefully to find the sentence ending(s). Mark where each full stop should go.

the dragon stepped out of its cave. it opened its mouth and gave a fiery breath.

3 Check that each sentence makes sense on its own.

the dragon stepped out of its cave.
it opened its mouth and gave a fiery breath.

4 Add capital letters to the first word of each sentence.

T   I
~~t~~he dragon stepped out of its cave. ~~i~~t opened its mouth and gave a fiery breath.

5 Check if there are any names of people, places or brands in the sentence that would also need a capital letter.

No, there are not.

6 Check your answer.

The dragon stepped out of its cave. It opened its mouth and gave a fiery breath.

Try this

1 Add a tick ✔ in each row to show what kind of **punctuation** is needed.

Sentence	?	!	.
What a lovely cake			
What time does the race start			
When you see Mark, please give him this letter			

2 Add two **full stops** and two **capital letters** to the passage below.

a mouse appeared on the table charlie ran out of the kitchen

3 Rewrite the sentence below adding correct **capital letters** and **punctuation**.

where is ben

_____

4 Underline the words that should have **capital letters** in the sentence below.

My brother, william, works for a large company called apple in america.

5 Which of the sentences below could use an **exclamation mark**?

Tick **one**.

I will meet you at break time ☐

How dreadful ☐

Please write your name at the top of the page ☐

Are you ready ☐

6 Add the correct **punctuation** to the sentences below.

Where do you live _____

Wherever we go, we always enjoy ourselves _____

When will we arrive _____

When we arrive, I want to explore _____

What a lucky goal _____

Top tip

• Remember that all parts of proper nouns (e.g. *Sally Smith, United Kingdom, Rising Stars Limited*) need capital letters.

Commas

To achieve 100 you need to use **commas** to mark clauses or phrases.

 ## What you need to know

- **Commas** are used to separate items in a list and to mark phrases or clauses.

Let's practise

Add a **comma** in the correct place to the sentence below.

After you have finished washing your hands you can have your breakfast.

1 Read the question and read it again. What is it asking?

The question is asking you to find where a comma should go.

2 Read the sentence carefully to find where the clauses meet.

There are two parts to this sentence and they meet after *hands*.

3 Check that one part makes sense on its own.

After you have finished washing your hands ✘ *you can have your breakfast.* ✔

4 Write the comma in the gap between *hands* and *you*.

After you have finished washing your hands, you can have your breakfast.

5 Check whether there is a list in the sentence.

No, there is no list.

6 Check your answer.

After you have finished washing your hands, you can have your breakfast.

Try this

1 Tick ✔ two boxes to show where the **commas** should go in the sentence below.

My favourite sports are football basketball tennis and athletics.
⬆ □   ⬆ □   ⬆ □   ⬆ □ ⬆ □

2 Add a **comma** to the sentence below.

Although Alma loves hamsters she is afraid of mice.

3 Tick ✔ to show which sentence contains correctly placed **commas**.

Tick **one**.

Ashton lives in, America. □

Mr Moreton, who is our new teacher, is great fun. □

Stephanie plays guitar, piano, and violin. □

If Marcus runs, his best he will win the race. □

4 Add one **comma** to the sentence below.

Running as fast as they could the children escaped from the dragon's lair.

5 Explain why a **comma** is used in the sentence below.

My dog likes chasing a ball, learning new tricks and sleeping by the fire.

_____

6 Tick ✔ two boxes to show where **commas** are used correctly in the sentences below.

Tick **two**.

Although we have studied this, before I can't remember much about it. □

If you like, we can get some pizza for supper. □

Unless you get up early, you will miss seeing the sun rise over the mountain. □

When you were little you used to do, funny little dances. □

Top tips

- In a sentence that contains a relative clause (see page 28), the information between the commas does not make sense on its own.
- In sentences that contain other types of subordinating conjunctions (see pages 24–25 and 29), the information on one side of a comma makes sense on its own. The information on the other side of the comma does not make sense on its own.
- There should be no comma before the last item in a list.

Inverted commas

To achieve 100 you need to use **inverted commas** to show speech.

✔ What you need to know

- **Inverted commas** are sometimes called speech marks. Inverted commas are put around what the speaker says.

I love swimming.

This is written as:
Daisy said, "I love swimming."
Or, "I love swimming," said Daisy.

- A new speech sentence starts with a capital letter (even if it is in the middle of another sentence). *Daisy asked, "Would anyone like to go swimming?"*
- Separate what was said from the speaker with a comma, unless there is a ? or an !.
- If the speech is at the beginning of the sentence, put a comma after what is said. *That was funny, said Freddie*
  Then, put the speech and the comma inside the inverted commas. *"That was funny," said Freddie.* Add a full stop at the end of the sentence.
- If the speech is at the end of the sentence put a comma after *said* (or whichever verb is used, e.g. *shouted, answered*). *Gemma said, I love a joke*
  Put a full stop at the end of the sentence. *Gemma said, I love a joke.*
  Add the inverted commas around what is said, including the full stop at the end. *Gemma said, "I love a joke."*

★ Let's practise

Tick ✔ two boxes to show where the **inverted commas** should go in the sentence below.

I'm hungry , said Emily .
⬆   ⬆   ⬆⬆   ⬆
☐   ☐☐   ☐

1 Read the question and read it again. What is it asking?

The question is asking you to find where the inverted commas should go.

2 Inverted commas go around the spoken words. Which words are spoken?

I'm hungry is spoken by Emily.

3 Tick the boxes around the spoken words. Make sure the punctuation goes **inside** the inverted commas.

Tick before *I'm* and after *hungry,*.

4 Check your answer.

I'm hungry , said Emily .
⬆   ⬆ ⬆   ⬆
✔   ☐ ✔   ☐

 **Try this**

1 Tick ✔ the boxes to show where the **inverted commas** should go in the sentence below.

How old are you? asked the policeman.

□   □   □   □

2 Add one comma and one full stop to each of the sentences below.

"My sister is a champion dancer " boasted Archie

Lucia added " My brother can dance well too "

3 Tick ✔ one box to show the sentence that is correctly punctuated.

Tick **one**.

"Let's play one of your computer games," suggested Amelie.   □

"Look at that elephant directed Mr Archer."   □

"Shall we go out in the rain"? asked the children.   □

I love playing in the rain," said Emily".   □

4 Rewrite the sentence below adding correct **punctuation**.

We won the match shouted the team

_____

5 Why are **inverted commas** used in the sentence below?

"Would you like to come for a walk?" asked Madeleine.

_____

6 Rewrite the sentence below using correct **punctuation** and **capital letters**.

Jacob shouted get out of the way.

_____

Apostrophes

To achieve 100 you need to use **apostrophes** correctly.

✔ What you need to know

- **Apostrophes** are used in two different ways:
  - To mark the place of a missing letter when we use **contractions**:
    I have got a good idea. = I've got a good idea.
    This is called the apostrophe of omission / contraction.
  - To show that something belongs to someone or something. This is called the **possessive apostrophe**, or the apostrophe of possession / ownership.
    - When something belongs to one person or thing, add an *s* and place the apostrophe before the *s*: *Beth's idea.*
    - When something belongs to plural persons or things, add the apostrophe after the last letter of the owners: *the foxes' hole.*

★ Let's practise

Rewrite the sentence below using a **contraction**.
Please do not walk on the grass.

1 Read the question and read it again. What is it asking? | The question is asking you to find which words can be contracted, and to write the contraction using an apostrophe.

2 Look for words that can be contracted. | *do not*

3 Write the contraction using an apostrophe to mark the missing letter. | *don't*

4 Check that no other words should be contracted. | There are none.

5 Check your answer. | Please don't walk on the grass.

Try this

1 Change the examples below to include a **possessive apostrophe**.

Example: *the coat that belongs to Jane = Jane's coat*

a) the sandwiches belonging to Casper

_____

b) the sail belonging to the boat

_____

c) the toys belonging to the children

_____

d) the friends of Alisha

_____

e) the ball belonging to the girl

_____

f) the games belonging to the girls

_____

2 Write the words below as **contractions**.

he does not   _____

she would not   _____

you should not   _____

3 Circle two words that should have **apostrophes** in the sentence below.

I didnt think itd be possible to do that.

4 Rewrite the sentence below using two correct **apostrophes**.

I cant see Jims picture from here.

_____

5 Rewrite the underlined word using a correct **apostrophe**.

Mrs Swain found the <u>childrens</u> pens scattered all over the floor.

_____

Top tips

- **Watch out:** *Its* and *It's* can be confusing. *It's* is only ever used to shorten *It is*. *Its* is used for possession. There is never an apostrophe used in *Its* for possession because it is a pronoun, like *his* or *her*.
- Nouns that refer to a group need a final s to show possession. Then, place the apostrophe before that s, e.g. *children's*, *herd's*, *people's*.

Parenthesis

To achieve 100 you need to recognise the correct use of a **parenthesis**.

✔ What you need to know

- A **parenthesis** is an 'extra' part of the sentence. The sentence can make sense without it. There are three forms of punctuating parenthesis: commas, **brackets** and **dashes**.
- A parenthesis can be used to:
  - give examples: *Goats will eat almost anything (grass, vegetables, bits of rubbish);*
  - add information: *Bats, a protected species, must not be killed.*
  - add a comment: *Edward – late as usual – finally arrived at school.*

Let's practise

Tick ✔ **two** boxes to show where **brackets** should go in the sentence below.

Carissa led the girls our best ever netball team onto the pitch.
  ☐ ☐

1 Read the question and read it again. What is it asking? | The question is asking you to identify the part of the sentence which should be in brackets.

2 Find the 'extra' information in the sentence. | *our best ever netball team* is extra information about *the girls*. This can be placed between brackets.

3 Check that you have ticked two boxes. | Carissa led the girls our best ever netball team onto the pitch.
☐ ✔ ✔ ☐

🖊 Try this

1 Underline the part of the sentence that could be placed in **parenthesis**.
Jena wanted her favourite breakfast toast, marmalade and ice-cream every day.

2 Rewrite the sentence below using two **commas**.
We visited Paris the capital of France on our holiday.

_____

3 Tick ✔ **two** boxes to show where the dashes should go in the sentence below.
Mr Hughes you wouldn't believe it can jump over a table even though he's sixty.
☐ ☐ ☐ ☐

Colons, semi-colons, single dashes, hyphens and bullet points

To achieve 100 you need to identify and use punctuation correctly.

✔ What you need to know

- Colons, semi-colons and single dashes can all be used to mark the boundary between independent clauses. They make a link between two sentences with linked ideas. Colons can be used to introduce a list.
- Hyphens are used to link two words together to make a compound noun.
- Bullet points are used to mark items in a list, which is introduced by a colon.

Let's practise

Add a **semi-colon** to the passage below.

Ross didn't want to go swimming he was afraid of going under the water.

1 Read the question and read it again. What is it asking?

The question is asking you to identify where a semi-colon should be used.

2 Find the two parts of the sentence and put a pencil mark where you think they meet.

Ross didn't want to go swimming / he was afraid of going under the water.

3 Check that each part of the sentence makes sense on its own. If they do, add the semi-colon.

Ross didn't want to go swimming; he was afraid of going under the water.

★ Try this

1 Draw a line to match the symbol with the name.

;		colon
:		semi-colon
—		dash

2 Add a **dash** to the sentence below.

It's your birthday tomorrow I know you will have lots of fun.

! Top tip

- Test questions may ask you to identify when these types of punctuation have been used correctly or incorrectly.

Prefixes and suffixes

To achieve 100 you need to know how to add **prefixes** and **suffixes** to words.

What you need to know

- **Prefixes** are added at the beginning of a root word (see page 55), and **suffixes** at the end of a root word to make a new word. (See also pages 55–59 for spelling rules about prefixes and suffixes.)
- Prefixes usually change the meaning of a word (e.g. *agree – disagree*).
- Suffixes usually change a word's form (e.g. an adjective to a noun: *clever – cleverness*).

Let's practise

Circle the **prefix** from the box that can be added to both of the words below.

| re- dis- mis- un- | ___appear   ___satisfied |

1 Read the question and read it again. What is it asking?

> The question is asking you to select the correct prefix that can be added to both words.

2 Try out each prefix with both words to find the one that makes sense.

> *reappear* ✔ *resatisfied* ✘. Re- is not the answer. *disappear* ✔ *dissatisfied* ✔.

3 Check the other options.

> *misappear* ✘ *missatisfied* ✘ *unappear* ✘ *unsatisfied* ✔. So, *dis* is the answer.

4 Check your answer.

> re (dis) mis un

Try this

1 Make new words by adding a correct **prefix** or **suffix** to these words.

Prefixes: **un- dis- re- sub-**   *Suffixes*: **-ness -ment -ful -ly**

conscious   agree   forgive   hate   like   arrange   organise

_____

_____

2 Circle one **prefix** that can be added to both of these words.

dis- mis- un- pre-   ___understand   ___take

3 Underline the **suffixes** in the words below.

employment   respectful   faster   thoughtless

Prefixes

To achieve 100 you need to correctly spell words with **prefixes**.

✓ What you need to know

- Most prefixes are added to the beginning of root words without any changes in spelling. So, if a word begins with the same letter as the end of the prefix, both letters are used (e.g. *dis* + satisfy = di*ss*atisfy, *un* + necessary = u*nn*ecessary).
- Some prefixes have negative meanings (e.g. *dis* + appoint, *mis* + behave, *un* + do).
- Do not to confuse *dis* and *des*:
  - When a word begins with *dis*, you can usually remove *dis* and a root word will still exist (e.g. *disappear* = *dis* + appear).
  - When a word begins with *des*, it doesn't usually make sense if you remove the *des* (e.g. *despise*, *describe*).
- *in* means 'not' before words beginning with most letters, except:
  - before a root word starting with *l*, *in* becomes *il*;
  - before a root word starting with *m* or *p*, *in* becomes *im*;
  - before a root word starting with *r*, *in* becomes *ir*.
- Prefixes can be used for a range of meanings:
  re = again or back   *sub* = under   *inter* = between
  super = above   *anti* = against   *auto* = self

★ Try this

Use the rules above and the *Let's practise* flowchart on page 54 to help you answer the following questions.

1 Write the words below adding a correct **prefix**.
  agree   tidy   obey   behave   do   lead

2 Add the words to the table in the correct column, including the **prefix**.
  correct   mature   patient   responsible   possible   regular   legal

in	im	il	ir

! Top tip

- Remember to keep the double letter if the prefix ends and the word begins with the same letter.

55

Suffixes: -*tion*, -*ssion*, -*cian*

To achieve 100 you need to correctly spell words with these **suffixes**.

✓ What you need to know

- The sound 'shun' at the end of words can be spelled in different ways.
  - -*tion* is the most common spelling of the 'shun' sound. It is used if the root word ends in *t* or *te* (e.g. inven<u>t</u> = *invention*).
  - -*sion* is used if the word ends in *d* or *se* (e.g. revi<u>se</u> = *revision*, expan<u>d</u> = *expansion*).
  - -*cian* is used if the root word ends in *c* or *cs* (e.g. *musician*). These words often refer to a person's job.
  - -*ssion* is used if the root word ends in *ss* or *mit* (e.g. express = *expression*, permit = *permission*).

✎ Try this

Use the rules above to help you answer the following questions.

1 Underline the final letters of the root words, looking at the correct use of the **suffix**. Look, cover, say and write.

Root word	'shun' suffix	Look, cover, say and write
inject	injection	_____
comprehend	comprehension	_____
hesitate	hesitation	_____

2 Add -<u>ian</u> to make the word for the job. Then, look, cover, say and write.

electric___   magic___   politic___   mathematic___   optic___

3 Rewrite these words including the **suffix** -<u>ssion</u>.

express _____   discuss _____   confess _____

! Top tips

- Remember to remove the final letter before the suffix, if necessary.
- Think 'Ian' has lots of jobs. So use -*ian* if the word is a job.

Suffixes: -ous, -tious, -cious

To achieve 100 you need to correctly spell words with these **suffixes**.

What you need to know

- Sometimes the root word is obvious (e.g. poison + -ous = *poisonous*).
- But sometimes there is no root word, so learn these common words: *enormous, fabulous, jealous, tremendous, obvious*. Look, cover, say and write.
- When adding suffixes to words ending with a vowel or *y*:
  - If the root ends in e, remove it before adding *ous*: fame = remove e = *famous*.
  - If the root ends in y, change it to *i* before adding *ous*: vary = y becomes *i* = *various*.
  - If there is an ee sound before the *ous* ending, it is usually spelled as *i* (e.g. *serious, obvious, curious*).
- A few words have e before *ous* (e.g. *hideous, spontaneous, courteous*).
- *-our* changes to *-or* before *-ous* is added (e.g. humour = humor = *humorous*).
- The sound 'shus' at the end of words can be spelled in different ways (e.g. *-tious, -cious*).
- If the root word ends in ce the 'shus' sound is usually spelled as *-cious* (e.g. grace = *gracious*).
- If the root words ends in *-tion*, the 'shus' sound is usually spelled as *-tious* (e.g. ambition = *ambitious*). Exception: *anxious*.

Try this

Use the rules above and the *Let's practise* flowchart on page 54 to help you answer the following questions.

1 Add the correct **suffix** and change the spelling to:

glamour ＿＿＿＿＿＿

2 Change the y to i and add the **suffix** -<u>ous</u> to the words below:

vary ＿＿＿＿＿＿

fury ＿＿＿＿＿＿

glory ＿＿＿＿＿＿

3 Add the correct **suffix** and change the spelling to these words ending in -ce.

grace ＿＿＿＿＿＿

space ＿＿＿＿＿＿

Suffixes: -able, -ably, -ible, -ibly

To achieve 100 you need to correctly spell words with these **suffixes**.

✔ What you need to know

- The *-able/-ably* ending is the most common spelling of this type of suffix.
- It is usually used when a complete root word can be heard before it
  (e.g. depend = *dependable*).
- It is also used with root words that can also have the ending *-tion*
  (e.g. application = *applicable*).
- If the root word ends in *-ce* or *-ge*, the final e is kept (e.g. change = *changeable*).
  Exception: force = *forcible*.
- The *-ible* ending is often used when a complete root word can't be heard before
  it (e.g. *possible/possibly*). Exception: *sensible*.

Try this

Use the rules above and the *Let's practise* flowchart on page 54 to help you answer the following questions.

1 Rewrite the words below into two groups.

adorably   noticeable   understandably   enjoyable   terribly   horrible   comfortable

Complete root word can be heard (-able/-ably)	No root word (-ible/-ibly)

2 Rewrite the words below, adding -<u>able</u> and -<u>ably</u>. The first one is done for you.

Root word	-*able*	-*ably*
pity	pitiable	pitiably
rely		
identify		
envy		

Suffixes: *-ant, -ance, -ancy, -ent, -ence, -ency*

To achieve 100 you need to correctly spell words with these **suffixes**.

What you need to know

- A word with an *-ant* suffix spelling will also have an *-ance* and *-ancy* suffix if these forms of the word exist (e.g. important = *importance*).
- A word with an *-ent* suffix spelling will also have an *-ence* and *-ency* suffix if these forms of the word exist (e.g. evident = *evidence*).
- The *-ant, -ance, -ancy* suffixes are used after root words that can also have *-ation* endings (e.g. expect = expectation = *expectant*; hesitation = *hesitant*; toleration = *tolerance*).
- The *-ent, -ence, -ency* suffixes are used with words that have the following sounds:
  - soft *c* (e.g. *decency, innocence, licence, magnificent, complacent*);
  - soft *g* (e.g. *intelligence, urgent, emergency*);
  - *qu* (e.g. *frequency, sequence, consequence*).
- However, there are exceptions and these words just have to be learned. For example:

  independence   obedient   independent   sentence   silence   violence
  influence   assistant   performance   balance   appearance   distance

Try this

Use the rules above and the *Let's practise* flowchart on page 54 to help you answer the following questions.

1 Read this short passage and find the <u>-ent</u>, <u>-ence</u> or <u>-ency</u> words and the <u>-ant</u>, <u>-ance</u> or <u>-ancy</u> words. Sort them into two groups.

> The whole room was silent as the performance was about to commence. The acrobat was going to balance upon a high wire holding a magnificent crystal glass. Her appearance shocked the audience as she was no more than a small child. An assistant lifted her up to the wire and she began to cross the distance between the two posts.

-ent, -ence, -ency words	-ant, -ance, -ancy words

2 Write the missing word endings in this quick quiz.

   a) The young horse was hesit_____ about approaching the people.

   b) Please be quick. This is an emerg_____.

   c) Listen. This is very import_____.

59

Words with *ei, eigh, ey, ay*

To achieve 100 you need to correctly spell words with these combinations of letters.

✔ What you need to know

- The long *ai* sound is spelled in a number of ways: *ei, eigh, ey* or *ay*. You must know which words use which groups of letters.

★ Try this

1 Complete the sentences using the **correct spelling**.

a) The person who lives next to me is my ＿＿＿＿＿＿＿＿.　　neighbour / nieghbour

b) I love to slide on a ＿＿＿＿＿＿＿ in the snow.　　sley / sleigh

c) My dog ＿＿＿＿＿＿＿ my commands.　　obays / obeys

Words with *ie, ei*

✔ What you need to know

- Many words are spelled with *ie* to make the long *ee* sound. However, there are exceptions: *friend, fierce*
- The '*i* before *e* except after *c*' rule works for words where the sound after the *c* is a long *e* sound (e.g. *receive, deceive*). However, there are other words where the *ei* spelling does not say the long *ee* sound (e.g. *ancient, either, neither, leisure, seize, their*).

★ Try this

Use the rules above and the *Let's practise* flowchart on page 54 to help you answer the following questions.

1 Add <u>ie</u> or <u>ei</u> to the words below.

a) ach＿＿ve　　c) rec＿＿pt

b) sh＿＿ld　　d) n＿＿ce

2 Copy these words into an <u>ie</u> group and an <u>ei</u> group, then use each word in a sentence.

mischief neither pierce seize deceive grief piece siege science
field friend

Words with *ough*

To achieve 100 you need to correctly spell words with this combination of letters.

✔ What you need to know

- The *ough* spelling is used for many different sounds:

Sound	or	uff	long *o* (owe)	oo	off	short *u*	ow
Example	bought	tough	though	through	cough	thorough	plough

⭐ Let's practise

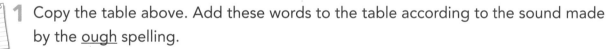

Add the correct <u>ough</u> word to complete the sentence.

Think hard and give the problem some _____.

1 Read the question and read it again. What is it asking?

The question is asking you to add an *ough* word to the sentence.

2 Think of what *ough* words you know. Which word would make sense in the sentence?

The word could be *thought*.

3 Check the sentence makes sense and the spelling of the word is correct.

Think hard and give the problem some <u>thought</u>.

⭐ Try this

1 Copy the table above. Add these words to the table according to the sound made by the <u>ough</u> spelling.

thought   enough   rough   nought   although   bough   ought   coughing   thoughtful

2 Write a sentence to explain what each of these words means.

bough

dough

trough

plough

Word endings: *al, el, il, le*

To achieve 100 you need to correctly spell words with these letters at the ends.

✔ What you need to know

- The *le* spelling is the most common spelling for the sound /ə +l/ at the end of words. Nearly three quarters of words with this sound are spelled with *le*: *table, apple, bottle, little, middle, style.*
- Not many nouns end in *al* but many adjectives do. Learn the commonly used nouns: *metal, pedal, capital, hospital, animal.*
- Adjectives: *accidental, alphabetical, additional, chemical, colossal, final, national.*
- The *el* spelling is used after words ending with *m, n, r, v, w* and often after *s*: *camel, tunnel, squirrel, travel, towel, tinsel.*
- Not many words end in *il* so learn the commonly used ones that do: *pencil, fossil, nostril, daffodil, devil.*

Let's practise

Complete each word with the l<u>e</u> or <u>e</u>l spelling.

rumb_____   cam_____

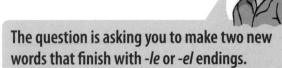

1   Read the question and read it again. What is it asking?

The question is asking you to make two new words that finish with *-le* or *-el* endings.

2   Remind yourself which letters tell you when to use *el*: *m, n, r, v, w* and *s*. Then try the *el* ending for that word. Try the *le* ending for the other word.

rumb<u>le</u> ✔
cam<u>el</u> ✔

3   Check your answer.

rumble   camel

Try this

1   Decide whether the word beginnings below will use the l<u>e</u> or <u>e</u>l spelling.

a) marb_____   c) possib_____   e) jew_____

b) beet_____   d) swiv_____   f) cocker_____

2   Add <u>al</u> to these words to make them adjectives.

a) music_____   b) critic_____   c) tropic_____   d) tradition_____

Silent letters

To achieve 100 you need to correctly spell words with **silent letters**.

✔ *What you need to know*

- **Silent letters** appear in the spelling of a word, but are not heard when the words are spoken.
- You will need to learn common words with silent letters.

★ *Let's practise*

Circle the **silent letter** in each of the words below.
knuckle   knee   wrist

1 Read the question and read it again. What is it asking?

The question is asking you to find the letter in each word that is silent.

2 Read each word. Which letters can't be heard?

knuckle – you can't hear the *k*; knee – you can't hear the *k*; wrist – you can't hear the *w*.

3 Check you have circled all the silent letters.

Ⓚnuckle   Ⓚnee   Ⓦrist

✗ *Try this*

1 Match these words containing **silent letters** with the pictures. Write a passage using as many words with silent letters as you can.

lamb / lam
thisle / thistle
knight / night
island / iland
autum / autumn
sine / sign
ghost / gost
guard / gard
bom / bomb
column / colum

a

b

c

d

e

f

g

h

i

j

2 Write your own sentences using the words with **silent letters** below.

I don't <u>know</u> the <u>answer</u> so I shall <u>guess</u> it. I hope I don't get it <u>wrong</u>. Yippee, I have <u>written</u> it correctly.
To be <u>honest</u>, I <u>doubt</u> that I can arrive in an <u>hour</u>.

Homophones

To achieve 100 you need to correctly spell a variety of **homophones**.

 ## What you need to know

- **Homophones** are words that sound the same but have different meanings.
- Some of the most common homophones are:
    - *there, their* and *they're*
    - *your* and *you're*
    - *to, too* and *two*.

Let's practise

Add the correct spelling of the word in the gap.

they're / their / there
↓

Please put your bags over _____.

1 Read the question and read it again. What is it asking?

The question is asking you to add the correct homophone to finish the sentence.

2 Check the easiest option to spot. Would *they are* make sense?

Put your bags over *they are*. ✘

3 Check if it could be something that belongs to someone, even if it is not a visible thing, e.g. Their ideas are great.

The sentence is not about ownership. Put your bags over *their*. ✘

4 If it is not the other two options, the answer must be *there*.

Please put your bags over ___there___.

5 Check that the sentence makes sense.

Top tip

- Use a method to check which spelling you need. Do not guess.
  They're = They are
  Their   = belonging to them
  There   = indicates a place

 **Try this**

1 Use <u>they're</u>, <u>their</u> or <u>there</u> to complete the sentences below.

a) At the zoo, _____ was a giraffe.

b) Josh and Jen are going on holiday. _____ very lucky.

c) They have left _____ coats on the bus.

d) The magician told the audience that he could read _____ thoughts.

2 Circle the **homophone** in each sentence.

Are you allowed to come out to play?	I thought of the answer and then said it aloud.
There is an aisle between the seats on a bus.	We live in the British Isles.
Our car had to brake hard to avoid hitting the dog.	Please don't break my new pencil.
Your house is farther away from school than mine.	Joe's father is a nurse.
We have a guest speaking in our assembly today.	I would never have guessed that Jill is only six years old.
We gave a groan of despair as it was raining again.	You have grown a lot this year.
Have you heard the news?	You are behaving like a herd of elephants.
William led the class on a treasure trail.	The core of the pencil is known as the lead.
In the past, people didn't have computers.	I passed my spelling test.
It would be lovely to have peace all over the world.	Can I have a piece of cake?
We must have a plain coloured coat for school.	I will fly on a plane for the first time.
The weather is wonderful today.	I don't know whether to have a blue or red bike.

3 Add <u>your</u> or <u>you're</u> to the gaps.

_____ kind to invite me but I can't come to _____ house today because _____ mum said that _____ all going to visit the dentist.
I hope you have cleaned _____ teeth.

4 Write the correct word and spelling.

a) I saw a h_____ of cows.

b) There is a lot of sand in a d_____.

c) I didn't know the answer so I g_____.

d) I can't believe you said that a_____.

Synonyms and antonyms

To achieve 100 you need to know the terms **synonym** and **antonym**, and identify examples.

✓ What you need to know

- **Synonyms** are words that have the same meaning.
- **Antonyms** are words that have opposite meanings.

Let's practise

Tick ✔ the words that mean the **opposite** of difficult:

tricky, challenging ☐   generous, helpful ☐

easy, simple ☐   rare, scarce ☐

1	Read the question and read it again. What is it asking?	The question is asking you to find words which mean the opposite of *difficult*.
2	Try out each pair of words to find the opposite of *difficult*.	*Tricky* and *challenging* mean the same as *difficult*; *generous* and *helpful*, *rare* and *scarce* are not linked to the word *difficult*; *easy* and *simple* are opposite to *difficult*.
3	Tick the correct box.	**easy, simple** ✔
4	Check your answer.	

Try this

1 Draw a line to match the **synonyms**.

clever		begin
attractive		punctual
awful		disgusting
prompt		beautiful
start		intelligent

2 Write an **antonym** for the words below.

love   _____

quiet   _____

comfortable   _____

modern   _____

! Top tips

- Remember: *S* for synonym, *S* for same. *A* for antonym, *A* for against (opposite to).
- Double-check the question to know whether you are looking for similar or opposite meanings.

Word families

To achieve 100 you need to know words that share the same root word or prefix.

What you need to know

- Many words are related in form and meaning; these are known as **word families**.
- Words that belong to a family usually share the same root word or prefix. For example:

  sign   signature   design

  auto   automatic   autobiography   autonomous

  science   scientific

  conscience   unconscious

Let's practise

> Circle three words that belong to the same **word family**.
> bicycle   bison   cycle   reappear   recycle

1 Read the question and read it again. What is it asking?

The question is asking you to find three words with a common root word.

2 Which parts of words are repeated?

re is repeated twice. *bi* is repeated twice. *cycle* is repeated three times.

3 Check that the words you have chosen share a meaning.

Cycle, bicycle and *recycle* all contain the idea of turning through a process or position.

4 Check your answer.

(bicycle)   bison   (cycle)   reappear   (recycle)

Try this

1 Add another word to this **word family**.

patience

_____

2 Write the root word for this **word family**.

poster   postage   imposter

_____

3 Underline the two words that belong to the **word family** of <u>cent</u>, meaning one hundred.

ascent   centurion   century   descent   scented

Word list for Years 5 and 6

! **Top tips**

- Learn a few spellings each day.
- Use the look, cover, say and write method.
- Write sentences using these words.
- Look at the words and find other words within them (e.g. *independent* contains *in*, *depend*, *pen*, *dent*).

accommodate	embarrass	persuade
accompany	environment	physical
according	equip (-*ped*, -*ment*)	prejudice
achieve	especially	privilege
aggressive	exaggerate	profession
amateur	excellent	programme
ancient	existence	pronunciation
apparent	explanation	queue
appreciate	familiar	recognise
attached	foreign	recommend
available	forty	relevant
average	frequently	restaurant
awkward	government	rhyme
bargain	guarantee	rhythm
bruise	harass	sacrifice
category	hindrance	secretary
cemetery	identity	shoulder
committee	immediate(ly)	signature
communicate	individual	sincere(ly)
community	interfere	soldier
competition	interrupt	stomach
conscience	language	sufficient
conscious	leisure	suggest
controversy	lightning	symbol
convenience	marvellous	system
correspond	mischievous	temperature
criticise (*critic* + *ise*)	muscle	thorough
curiosity	necessary	twelfth
definite	neighbour	variety
desperate	nuisance	vegetable
determined	occupy	vehicle
develop	occur	yacht
dictionary	opportunity	
disastrous	parliament	

Glossary

Active voice The sentence form that uses subject + verb order.

Adjective A word that describes a noun.

Adverb A word that adds information to a verb.

Adverbial A word or phrase that adds information about a verb.

Antonym A word that is an opposite of another.

Apostrophe A punctuation mark that is used to replace a letter in a contracted word, or to indicate possession.

Brackets Punctuation marks that are used to show parenthesis.

Bullet point A punctuation mark used to identify items in a vertical list.

Capital letter An upper case letter.

Colon A punctuation mark that is used to introduce a list or an explanation or conclusion.

Comma A punctuation mark that is used to separate clauses within a sentence.

Command A sentence type that gives an instruction or order.

Conjunction A word or phrase that is used to join two clauses within a sentence.

Contraction A word form in which an apostrophe is used to replace a letter or letters.

Coordinating conjunction A word that joins one main clause to another main clause.

Dash A punctuation mark that can be used singly to introduce a dependent clause or phrase, or in pairs to indicate parenthesis.

Determiner A word which introduces a noun, e.g. a, the.

Exclamation A sentence type that indicates an emotional expression, e.g. shock, delight.

Exclamation mark A punctuation mark that indicates an emotional expression, e.g. shock, delight.

Full stop A punctuation mark that indicates the end of a sentence.

Homophone A word whose pronunciation has more than one meaning, e.g. hear, here.

Hyphen A symbol of punctuation that is used to combine two words, e.g. quick-minded.

Inverted commas Punctuation marks, also called speech marks, that are used to indicate direct speech.

Main clause A part of a sentence that is not dependent upon other parts of the sentence to make sense.

Modal verb A word that is used in combination with another verb to indicate probability or obligation.

Noun A word that describes an object or abstract idea.

Noun phrase A group of words which gives information about and is dependent upon the noun.

Object A word or words that refer to the person or thing to which a verb is done.

Parenthesis A part of a sentence that contains information that is not integral to the meaning of that sentence.

Passive voice A sentence type in which the subject of the verb is not known, or not important and so the action or object of the verb becomes the focus.

Past perfect tense A verb form often used to make comparison between events in the historic past, prior to an event in the more recent past, e.g. He had opened the box before I could stop him.

Past progressive tense A verb form composed of the verb 'be' and a verb form ending in -ing to indicate an action that happened continuously in the past, e.g. I was running.

Past tense Verb forms that describe actions that happened in the past.

Plural This means 'more than one'.

Possessive apostrophe A punctuation mark used just before or just after the end of a noun to indicate that something belongs to that noun.

Prefix Letters that are added to the front of the word.

Preposition A word that indicates place or time; it is used within a noun phrase.

Present perfect tense A verb form that refers to an action begun in the past and continuing to the present.

Present progressive tense A verb form composed of the verb 'be' and a verb form ending in -*ing* to indicate an action that happens continuously in the present.

Present tense Verb forms that describe actions that happen in the present.

Pronoun A word that is used to substitute a noun.

Question A sentence type that asks for an answer.

Question mark A punctuation mark used to indicate that a sentence is a question.

Relative clause A group of words, including a verb, that provides information about a noun.

Semi-colon A punctuation mark that is used to indicate a relationship between two sentences.

Silent letter A letter that is used within the spelling of a word, but whose sound is not pronounced.

Singular This means 'one'.

Statement A sentence type that declares information.

Subject A word or words that indicate the person or thing performing the verb in a sentence.

Subjunctive verb form A verb form that is used to indicate the hypothetical nature of a verb, or to demonstrate formality.

Subordinate clause A group of words, including a verb, that is dependent upon the main clause in a sentence.

Subordinating conjunction A word or phrase that is used to introduce a subordinate clause.

Suffix A letter or letters that are added to the end of a word; it usually changes the word form, e.g. verb to noun: forgive – forgiveness.

Synonym A word that has the same, or very similar, meaning to another word.

Verb A word, or words, that describe an action or state.

Word family A group of words that has a common feature or pattern.

Answers

Nouns (page 8)
1 tick: sea
2 underline: Saturdays; park; garden
3 Accept any suitable noun, e.g. sisters; pets; toes.

Adjectives (page 9)
1 circle: favourite; new
2 N: kittens, cats; A: cuddly, playful
3 Accept a suitable clause including the word 'dangerous'. The answer must include a correctly placed full stop and any additional punctuation must be used correctly.

Verbs (page 10)
1 tick: sleeps
2 circle: fall; grow
3 underline: likes; is; made

Adverbs (page 11)
1 circle: silently; now
2 Accept the addition of any suitable adverb in a suitable location, e.g. Let's go home soon/now/later/slowly/quickly, or Quickly let's go home, or Let's quickly go home.

Modal verbs (page 13)
1 circle: must
2 tick: Jo may be singing in the show tonight.
3 Accept any suitable modal verb, e.g. can, may, should, might.
4 Susie will start school when she is four.   C
   Jake might come to our school.   P
   I can swim two lengths of the pool.   C
5 You will fall if you do that.
6 tick: If we all work together, we can be finished by lunchtime.
   When Colin arrives, he might show us his new game.

Adverbials (page 15)
1 tick: Later that day we all shared a pizza.
   We ran as fast as we could.
2 circle: by the end of the month
3 tick: in the new nature garden
4 Josh put on his coat more slowly than a snail. Correct punctuation must be used.
5 I'll meet you outside the swimming pool. tick: Where?
   Can you come at three o'clock? tick: When?
   After you have eaten your lunch, shall we play football? tick: When?
   Alisha clapped her hands at the same time as her sister. tick: When?

Pronouns (page 17)
1 tick: I love my pet rat.
   The children ate their lunches outside.
2 circle: you; I; your
3 He plays football.
4 tick: we; us
5 I; my; We
6 underline: He; it; his; he; it; it; him

Prepostions (page 19)
1 underline: to; on
2 tick: after; by
3 Accept any suitable preposition, e.g. under; below; by; next to; along.
4 circle: to; by; in
5 of; on
6 Accept the addition of any suitable preposition, e.g. Please put the boxes on/beside/beneath/below/next to the table.

7 circle: under; beside
8 on

Determiners (page 21)
1 an; a; an
2 tick: some; the
3 underline: any; the; these
4 Accept a numerical answer, e.g. two; four; or a determiner describing quantity, e.g. some; no; several; many; lots of.
5 tick: more; a

Statements, exclamations, commands and questions (page 23)
1 Now, please listen to the music.   C
   My computer is not working.   S
   It will be rainy today.   S
   Remember to bring your coats with you.   C
2 Accept any suitable question, e.g. Would you like a drink?/Shall I open the window?
3 Open the window.
4 Accept any suitable statement, e.g. I am going swimming./We want to play.
5 How awful!
   How do you do?
   What do you think?
   What a day!
6 What is your name?/Will you tell me your name?/Can you tell me your name?

Conjunctions (page 25)
1 while
2 tick: although
3 Accept any suitable coordinating conjunction that makes sense, e.g. and; so.
4 tick: We can play in the garden when we get home.
   Can you sing while you are playing the guitar?
   If you jump in the pool first, I will follow you.
5 Accept any suitable subordinating conjunction, e.g. because; as.
6 underline: since; so
7 Although/though; because/as

Main clauses and subordinate clauses (page 27)
1 tick: my favourite activity is going to the museum.
   My dad came into the room
2 tick: Freddie can run very well because he practises every day.
   When Oscar goes on holiday, he swims in the sea.
3 because; Although; if ·
4 circle: even though
5 underline: While you were playing outside; unless it rains.

Relative clauses (page 28)
1 circle: which was a large silver cup
2 Accept any suitable relative clause, either with or without a relative pronoun, e.g. who lives next door; called Alice.
3 underline: that was left outside the shop

Subordinating and coordinating conjunctions (page 29)
1 underline: although
2 if; even though; unless

Noun phrases (page 30)
1 tick: a; beautiful; cream; cake
2 Accept any suitable additions that make sense, e.g. Dino has a

great/new/exciting/computer/ board game.
3 underline: The shed at the end of the garden

Subject and object (page 31)
1 tick: Yuri plays tennis.
   We visit our cousins at the weekend.
2 circle: prize

Subject and verb agreement (page 33)
1 circle: is; wins
2 circle: prefers
3 tick: Beth and Ben want to be scientists.
   Wales is a country next to England.
4 circle: He
5 it: grows; does
   they: eat; believe

Verbs in the simple present and simple past tenses (page 35)
1 circle: played; danced
2 visited
3 Anna has two cats.
4 circle: went; climbed; bathed
5 circle: won
6 tick: went; made

Verbs in the progressive and perfect tenses (page 37)
1 tick: Archie is cooking tea for us.
   The children are waiting for their teacher.
2 underline: have lived
3 tick: were watching
4 are learning
5 had
6 Rob and Jamie are winning the game.   present progressive
   Shannon was jumping up and down with excitement.   past progressive
   My kittens were climbing up the curtains.   past progressive
   I am hiding under the table.
   present progressive

Passive and active voices (page 39)
1 tick: Trees had been knocked over by the wind.
2 Lola was playing tennis.   active
   The whole class loves basketball.   active
   The football match has been won by my class.   passive
   Many children in school want to learn to play rugby.   active
3 The prize was won by Hameed.

Subjunctive verb forms (page 41)
1 circle: sign
2 underline: arrive
3 tick: If I were you, I would save a little money each month.
4 were
5 start
6 were

Standard English and formality (page 43)
1 Jane <u>ain't</u> coming.   non-Standard English
   Hugh <u>was</u> ill yesterday.   Standard English
   I <u>done</u> my chores this morning.   non-Standard English
   We would like <u>them</u> ones, please. non-Standard English
2 circle: attempt; investigate
3 I haven't done anything wrong./I have done nothing wrong. Correct use of

71

capital letter, full stop and apostrophe (if necessary) is required.

Capital letters, full stops, exclamation marks and question marks (page 45)
1 What a lovely cake !
  What time does the race start   ?
  When you see Mark, please give him this letter   .
2 A mouse appeared on the table. Charlie ran out of the kitchen.
3 Where is Ben?
4 underline: william; apple; america
5 tick: How dreadful
6 Where do you live?
  Wherever we go, we always enjoy ourselves.
  When will we arrive?
  When we arrive, I want to explore.
  What a lucky goal!

Commas (page 47)
1 My favourite sports are football, basketball, tennis and athletics.
2 Although Alma loves hamsters, she is afraid of mice.
3 tick: Mr Moreton, who is our new teacher, is great fun.
4 Running as fast as they could, the children escaped from the dragon's lair.
5 Accept any suitable answer that refers to commas being used to separate items in a list, e.g. Commas are used in a list.
6 tick: If you like, we can get some pizza for supper.
  Unless you get up early, you will miss seeing the sun rise over the mountain.

Inverted commas (page 49)
1 "How old are you?" asked the policeman.
2 "My sister is a champion dancer," boasted Archie.
  Lucia added, "My brother can dance well too."
3 tick: "Let's play one of your computer games," suggested Amelie.
4 "We won the match," shouted the team.
5 Accept any suitable answer that refers to identifying what was said, e.g. They show what Madeleine actually said.
6 Jacob shouted, "Get out of the way."

Apostrophes (page 51)
1 a) Casper's sandwiches
  b) the boat's sail
  c) the children's toys
  d) Alisha's friends
  e) the girl's ball
  f) the girls' games
2 he doesn't; she wouldn't; you shouldn't
3 circle: didnt; itd
4 I can't see Jim's picture from here.
5 children's

Parenthesis (page 52)
1 underline: toast, marmalade and ice-cream
2 We visited Paris, the capital of France, on our holiday.
3 Mr Hughes, you wouldn't believe it, can jump over a table even though he's sixty.

Colons, semi-colons, single dashes, hyphens and bullet points (page 53)
1 ; semi-colon
  : colon
  – dash
2 It's your birthday tomorrow – I know you will have lots of fun.

Prefixes and suffixes (page 54)
1 conscious: unconscious; unconsciousness; sub-conscious; sub-consciousness; consciously; sub-consciously
  agree: agreement; disagree; disagreement
  forgive: forgiveness
  hate: hateful; hatefully
  like: unlike; unlikely; dislike; likeness; likely
  arrange: arrangement; disarrange; disarrangement
  organise: disorganise; re-organise
2 circle: mis
3 underline: ment; ful; er; less

Prefixes (page 55)
1 disagree; untidy/re-tidy; disobey; misbehave; undo/redo; mislead
2 in: correct
  im: mature; patient; possible
  il: legal
  ir: responsible; regular

Suffixes: -tion, -ssion, -cian (page 56)
1 t; d; e
2 electrician; magician; politician; mathematician; optician
3 expression; discussion; confession

Suffixes: -ous, -tious, -cious (page 57)
1 glamorous
2 various; furious; glorious
3 gracious; spacious

Suffixes: -able, -ably, -ible, -ibly (page 58)
1 Complete root word can be heard: adorably; noticeable; understandably; enjoyable; comfortable
  No root word: terribly; horrible
2 reliable; reliably
  identifiable; identifiably
  enviable; enviably

Suffixes: -ant, -ance, -ancy, -ent, -ence, -ency (page 59)
1 -ent, -ence, -ency words: silent; commence; magnificent; audience
  -ant, -ance, -ancy words: performance; balance; appearance; assistant; distance
2 a) hesitant
  b) emergency
  c) important

Words with ei, eigh, ey, ay (page 60)
  a) neighbour
  b) sleigh
  c) obeys

Words with ie, ei (page 60)
1 a) achieve
  b) shield
  c) receipt
  d) niece
2 ei: neither; seize; deceive
  ie: mischief; pierce; grief; piece; siege; science; field; friend
  Accept any appropriate sentences.

Words with ough (page 61)
1 or: bought; thought; nought; ought; thoughtful
  uff: tough; enough; rough
  long o (owe): though; although
  oo: through
  off: cough; coughing
  short u: thorough
  ow: plough; bough
2 Accept any suitable answer, e.g.
  A bough is the branch/part of a tree.
  Dough is used to make bread.
  Animals feed out of a trough.

A plough is used to turn over the soil.

Word endings: al, el, il, le (page 62)
1 a) marble
  b) beetle
  c) possible
  d) swivel
  e) jewel
  f) cockerel
2 a) musical
  b) critical
  c) tropical
  d) traditional

Silent letters (page 63)
1 lamb   a
  thistle   f
  knight   g
  island   b
  autumn   h
  sign   c
  ghost   d
  guard   i
  bomb   j
  column   e
2 Accept any appropriate sentences.

Homophones (page 65)
1 a) there
  b) They're
  c) their
  d) their
2 allowed/aloud; aisle/Isles; brake/break; farther/father; guest/guessed; groan/grown; heard/herd; led/lead; past/passed; peace/piece; plain/plane; weather/whether
3 You're kind to invite me but I can't come to your house today because your mum said that you're all going to visit the dentist. I hope you have cleaned your teeth.
4 a) herd
  b) desert
  c) guessed
  d) aloud

Synonyms and antonyms (page 66)
1 clever   intelligent
  attractive   beautiful
  awful   disgusting
  prompt   punctual
  start   begin
2 love: hate
  quiet: loud; noisy
  comfortable: uncomfortable; painful
  modern: old; old-fashioned

Word families (page 67)
1 patience: patient; impatient; impatience; patiently; impatiently
2 post
3 underline: centurion; century